YOUR WORK and YOUR LIFE

YOUR WORK ~~OR~~ *and* YOUR LIFE

Towards a true win-win

KRIST PAUWELS

WHO LOOKS
OUTSIDE,
DREAMS

WHO LOOKS
INSIDE,
AWAKES

C.G. Jung

LET'S DO
BOTH

PREFACE

We live in a time of both societal and economic change. Everything is evolving at breakneck speed. All the while, we try to continue with our simple and age-old purpose: to create circumstances in which we can be happy. This applies to all areas of our lives. Perhaps it is time for us to look for new ways to achieve that goal. If we are to be in a position to reinvent the world, then we need to have the courage to innovate ourselves.

In any case, many people feel that existing ways of working and living together need to change. Not by developing grandiose new systems or theories but by endeavouring to put into practice simple methods that can have an immediate impact on our lives. This is the premise of this guide. It offers a number of practical tools that can be applied to your living and working environments. These tools should help you to unlock more potential in yourself.

The guide is based on a few basic principles that work if you apply them. You can use them as a private individual or as a company or organisation. These principles arose from the experience we have built up at our communications and coaching agency. Over the past fifteen years, we have assisted many people, companies, organisations and governmental departments. As a result, we have gained insight into the inner workings of businesses, got to know people inside out and were given the opportunity to work with all sorts of exciting teams – from the boardroom to the warehouse.

I have never tired of looking for ways to create new dynamics that ensure that every single one of us is able to grow to our own full potential. And this in a way that is good for the people around us, resulting in everyone experiencing a greater sense of peace, healthy self-awareness, happiness and connectedness to their own lives and jobs.

This book shares these insights and includes numerous case stories from our personal experience.

Enjoy the read, enjoy your work and enjoy your life!
Krist Pauwels

——

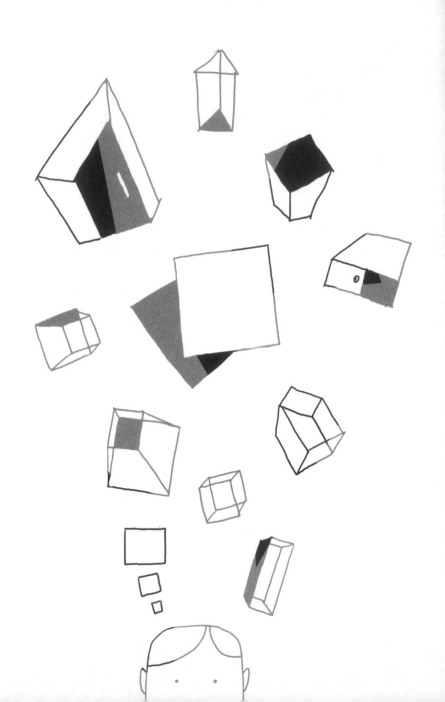

A TENDENCY TO COMPARTMENTALISE

In our effort to control the pressurised world around us, we are thinking more than ever in terms of compartments. We categorise people and situations. This helps us to pigeonhole a definite reality that furthermore matches our preconceptions. This is instinctive behaviour and as such is completely natural. If, for example, back in our prehistoric incarnation, we saw a predator, then we would quickly learn to put it into the compartment labelled "Dangerous" so that we would survive another day. One can see this behaviour in young children too: once they have ventured too close to something hot, in goes the experience into the "Be careful, hot!" compartment.

Our left hemisphere thus helps us to assess situations quickly and accurately. This is the side of our brain that creates order, sets limits, likes structure and is home to our self-awareness. The right side of our brain is intuitive, hungry for experience, more organic, associative and limitless in its consciousness.

If our modern society had a brain, it would be easy to conclude that the left hemisphere was more dominant than the right. Just look at the sciences. Rational and analytical thinking has made sure that people and the world are divided into more or less manageable research areas, each with its own particular features. As a result, we have made good progress in understanding our existence. We understand things better when we divide them into categories.

Of course, the original division was the one made between God and humanity. We have long represented God as a being separate from us, invisible and untouchable but nevertheless the one who defines who we are. The roots of many cultures are associated with a religion that makes this distinction. And since we have embraced this set-up, it has dictated our behaviour for centuries. Guilt, fear of omnipotence, awareness of our own nothingness: these are all firmly ingrained feelings that issue from the belief passed down to us for generations that God and ourselves belong in different compartments.

While we are often blissfully ignorant of it, this form of categorisation is at work in most areas of our lives. We frame situations by instantly labelling them so that they are comprehensible to us. Remarkably, we often behave the way that is expected of people in our compartment. We live up to the label that has been pinned on us and derive our identities from the boxes in which we find ourselves.

> WE LIVE UP TO THE LABEL THAT HAS BEEN PINNED ON US AND DERIVE OUR IDENTITIES FROM THE BOXES IN WHICH WE FIND OURSELVES.

Our personal compartment emphasises the fact that we are different to the others and as such defines who we are. This in turn creates a society that defines itself by difference and conflict rather than by similarity and agreement. It would seem that we have to struggle and fight to survive.

Take politics: are you a Christian democrat, a socialist, a liberal or a nationalist? Adopting a position at the intersection of these different political colours is not accepted as a valid basis for a political identity. Indeed, it is much easier and less ambiguous to instantly place someone in a compartment and to repeatedly stress their difference to other people. At home you are a father, a husband, a wife or a mother and you do what is expected in your category. We see the same divisions and tensions at work between the employer and the employee. There is no way around it: even in companies that increasingly assume a horizontal structure and experiment with new organisational systems, the distinction between top and down remains in place. For many, the

mentality persists that a certain distance is natural between the boss and the hired staff.

Another striking example of compartmentalisation in the work context is the so-called work-life balance. A popular topic, these days there is not a modern organisation that has not given it considerable thought and miles of print are devoted to the subject. Naturally, it is not a bad thing that we are encouraged to examine the way that we organise our lives. But in actual fact, this term is also predicated upon a distinction: it implies that on the one hand we have a life and on the other we have a job. As though the two could be separated. As if your working hours are something you have to do in order to have a life outside of those hours. This is patently absurd. We all have one life. Maybe we should be talking about balance in our lives – with work as an integral part of that.

IT IS STRIKING TO SEE HOW MANY PEOPLE, INCLUDING YOUNG PEOPLE, VIEW THEIR PROFESSIONAL PERSONA AS SEPARATE FROM THAT OF THEIR PRIVATE LIFE.

You may feel tempted to dismiss this argument as mere semantics. But in fact, it is very real. We live and behave within the context that we create for ourselves. It is striking to see how many people, including young people, view their professional persona as separate from that of their private life. But it would seem more sensible and less stressful if one could be 100 percent the same person in both areas of one's life. This is precisely where the secret lies to our further growth as human beings and society.

———

MACHOS, SMART GUYS AND HOTHEADS

If we go about dividing up reality into compartments we are also more likely to use the purely rational side of ourselves as a yardstick for decisions about our everyday survival in the jungle that is life. This means that even in our personal lives, the left hemisphere of our brains is going to dominate. Leaving little room for the right side, where feelings, intuition and experience are housed.

The work environment is an apt example of this. In most companies, there are two dimensions at work simultaneously: the visible, rational reality and the invisible realm of emotions. We often speak in this context of the reality "above the table" and "below the table".

Above the table is rational reality as we know it, in which we interact with our colleagues. You play the role that you are handed or which you give yourself. It is a role that dictates whether you do or do not speak in meetings, take or avoid initiatives, speak loudly or softly. You do what is expected of you and play the game of action and reaction. When people have worked together for a long time, this reality is stuck in a pattern of consensual behaviour. This structure allows everyone to feel more or less safe as they play their specific roles. Each individual inhabits their little compartment and acts accordingly. This often gives rise to caricatures in the workplace. Wherever you go, you will find the cheerful, the surly and the embattled colleague.

Here's a fun way to see how patterns have been established in your workplace: imagine you are the director of a TV series and you need to cast your colleagues in various roles. Who is the macho, who the hothead, who the reticent smart one, who is easy to tease (because he/she likes it), who the outcast and so forth. You will soon realise that it's relatively easy to typecast each of your colleagues. We all seek our compartments and conspire in this fabricated world of work.

However, this is, of course, only a part of the picture. People often experience themselves as very different than the person they present to the world. The reality below the table is a secret one of feelings, intuition and convictions that cannot breathe the rarefied air of rationality above the table. But it is essential for our well-being. And it guides our behaviour.

In an outside world built on reason, we have learned that it is not appropriate to show our innermost feelings. The deeper emotions that drive all human behaviour are often left to wither away in our unconscious or subconscious. We do not give this hidden reality a chance to surface, especially not in the workplace.

A man who was having difficulty processing the grief of a broken relationship showed himself to be exceptionally focused and efficient at work. It appeared as if he had more time than ever for his job, which of course was partly true. But he was also running from the hurt he felt. He received a lot of corroboration for his positive behaviour from his colleagues and management. Yet he felt increasingly empty. On a rational level, everything seemed great; emotionally, he was a wreck. There were small, telltale signs at work. The man didn't show up for lunch with his colleagues as often as before; he increasingly avoided other informal situations; and he looked more unkempt and smoked more heavily than he had previously. Fortunately, there was an observant HR manager who sensed that something was not quite right and spoke to him about it. The man was one step away from a complete burnout.

One can apply this story to the wider economic and political processes. Look at economics: for a long time, we considered it to be an exact science based purely on figures. More recently, we have started to see how an invisible, irrational world of speculation and inference is actually controlling it. We are still learning how to handle this fact.

Rational argumentation is also the foundation of politics. Yet no world leader would deny that it is the underlying emotional connections that decide whether an agreement is reached or, on the contrary, a conflict arises. It is therefore also useful for a community to examine what emotional traumas may still be at work in its collective unconscious. No matter what you may think, an underlying historical reality is often the driving force of a region's political and social life. For example, when, in the past, a region has felt suppressed by other regions with which it is now united in one country, it often demonstrates some form of nationalism or desire for independence. If the former aggressor then reacts from an unprocessed and unconscious past, then there will be acrimony once more, words will fall on deaf ears and there will be no real progress for the country.

———

EXPLORING THE HIDDEN WORLD

What does the "hidden world" actually look like? What exactly are the emotions buried "below the table"? If this unconscious and subconscious side of us is so important, it would seem reasonable to try to get to know it.

Sometimes it concerns emotions with which we are familiar but which we cannot ventilate in a calm manner at work. They may be easy to show, for example, when we get home or when we talk about work with friends. In this way, we use one social role to let off steam about another. If we could be present at family dinner tables all over the world, we would be confronted with a lot of emotions. These express themselves in gossip about, for example, the stupidity of one colleague, the disorderliness of another, the arrogance of the boss or the brilliance of a secretary who always saves the day. It is often a case of using archetypes to exaggerate in order to get frustrations out of our systems. And make no mistake: no one is spared from this sort of malicious talk.

Hidden feelings are also the breeding ground for those worries that keep us awake at night. You toss and turn, wake up earlier than usual in a sweat, your mind churning with scraps of information that it has stored in your subconscious during the day. Again, everything is magnified. Before you know it, you are telling yourself that you have lost your job just because your boss has not yet responded to an email. Or you are sure you have lost an important client because you forgot to call them. The night is a magnifying glass of your unconscious reality: a place where your imagination can cut loose without any shame. It is impressive to see how flawlessly our biological system works: our hidden insecurities, fears and repressed emotions – never allowed to see the light of day – are released to go on the rampage once it is dark.

THE NIGHT IS A MAGNIFYING GLASS OF YOUR UNCONSCIOUS REALITY: A PLACE WHERE YOUR IMAGINATION CAN CUT LOOSE WITHOUT ANY SHAME.

When we have too few of these escape routes at our disposal, it is natural that there will be breakdowns at work. Pent-up emotions will find their way out, often in the form of tantrums or a fit of tears. There is very little nuance in these moments.

Our hidden reality also manifests in the old and often deeply held convictions that we bring with us from our childhood. These beliefs influence every situation in which we find ourselves, usually without us being aware of it. This type of driver is based on imprints on our behavioural patterns. Imprints can be the result of traumatic experiences or simply the way we were raised.

For example, if someone was made to shoulder a lot of responsibility in the family in which they grew up, then they will be more likely to take the blame for situations in their adult environment. Or if someone was repeatedly told that they were worthless, in later life they will often compensate by trying to act strong. Thus we are all living with old, fixed beliefs that we cannot even remember but which dictate our behaviour.

When all those secret emotions and old convictions huddle together in the dark for long enough they tend to join forces to create a bunch of even deeper existential fears. These are the shadow areas of your personality, in front of which hangs a big sign: No Entry. This is precisely because the fears have grown so huge that they plumb your depths and may even have the nerve to call into question your right to exist.

Sometimes they dial up very deep, unresolved and repressed traumas. No wonder we do not go in search of them. On the contrary, we put a lot of energy into ignoring them in the hope of avoiding

WHEN ALL THOSE SECRET EMOTIONS AND OLD CONVICTIONS HUDDLE TOGETHER, THEY TEND TO JOIN FORCES TO CREATE A BUNCH OF EVEN DEEPER EXISTENTIAL FEARS.

any confrontation. This hidden level often asserts itself in fearful images that may also appear in nightmares. It is also the realm that can drive people over the edge. It is not so difficult per se to seek out your own unconscious fears. The simple question "What would drive me insane?" is a good start. This places little antennas in your psyche that can feel their way into your no-go zone.

'To have to always sit in a crowded, noisy place. That would drive me mad. But I don't see what that has to do with my subconscious shadow areas.' This was a comment from someone to whom I explained this concept. Her reaction is understandable because this is, after all, about a side of ourselves that we never see.

A simple way to explore our fears goes like this: imagine that you are in the situation that you wish to avoid (in this case, a crowded, noisy place) and try to actually live through it. Allow the feelings that it evokes to penetrate your nervous system. Ask yourself what fear it is that lurks under the surface and articulate that fear. Perhaps that could be, for example: "I'm afraid that I have no meaning and I might just vanish in the crowd", "I'm afraid of losing control of myself or of losing myself". Whatever emotion emerges, you are at least closer to the existential angst that is hidden in your unconscious.

A very extreme example of this is the case of an older woman who told me that as a small child during the Second World War, she spent three years incarcerated in a concentration camp with her mother. They endured unimaginable horrors. She survived and built a life. And she has stayed awake every night for years. If she sleeps, terrifying images from her past return. Only in the mornings does she allow herself to nod off. This beautiful and highly lucid woman understands perfectly well what is going on and says: 'I am reconciled to the fact that there are traumas that I can no longer come to terms with. I have made the choice to not visit my demons every night. And so, over and over again, I put a lot of energy into not letting myself go to sleep.'

When underlying emotions are not given an outlet, they often turn into physical complaints. The body is an incredibly important and powerful barometer of mental well-being and sends us signals when inner tensions have built up. People who work very hard can generally only sustain this by training their bodies: focused tension alternated with conscious relaxation.

WHEN UNDERLYING EMOTIONS ARE NOT GIVEN AN OUTLET, THE BODY IS AN INCREDIBLY IMPORTANT AND POWERFUL BAROMETER OF MENTAL WELL-BEING AND SENDS US SIGNALS WHEN INNER TENSIONS HAVE BUILT UP.

An osteopath explained to me how surprised he always is at how people can resolve emotional issues through their bodies. Physical therapy can touch on deep emotions. 'There is cursing and weeping in my practice,' he says, 'simply because massage releases certain tensions in the body. Sometimes it's about specific situations that people have experienced and need to let go of. But often the emotion is unclear and hard to pin down. In any case, the relief is always great afterwards.'

TIME FOR CREATIVITY

It is actually an absurd situation. In a world that is becoming increasingly complex to negotiate, we use only one facet of ourselves to survive. The crucial question is not why we fail to use our hidden energy reserves to get more out of our lives and work, but how we can turn this around.

Compare it with an iceberg. The part that sticks out of the water represents your outer world; the huge mass underneath symbolises the guiding energy that defines who you are. It takes a lot of effort for people to keep this concealed reality under the surface day in, day out. Because it is an unnatural state of affairs.

In my experience working with companies and organisations over the past fifteen years, I have invariably found that when people consciously address their under-the-table realities, face up to and share them with each other, the work situation instantly changes. New energy and creativity is tapped into, which makes you feel happier, better able to collaborate and to get more from the situations in which you find yourself. You no longer feel like a spectator watching a soap of your own life: instead you are at the centre of your story. You experience your life and your work. You feel that you are alive and that you are growing. In fact, you exit the mental framework and return to the broader experiential context. The right side of your brain is activated.

It goes without saying that this takes courage. As an individual, since you have to plumb your depths to find new creativity and energy. As a group, since you have to create the context in which this is even possible. It may seem like a daunting task, but it is anything but that. The fear of the emotion is always greater than the emotion itself. Furthermore, we have little choice. Today, many people feel as though the energy they need to keep their heads above water is gradually running out.

THE CRUCIAL QUESTION IS NOT WHY WE FAIL TO USE OUR HIDDEN ENERGY RESERVES TO GET MORE OUT OF OUR LIVES AND WORK, BUT HOW WE CAN TURN THIS AROUND.

An executive of a medium-sized company was a very driven person who pushed his team on a daily basis. He was a workaholic and seemed indomitable despite his increasing fatigue. He did admit that the pressure he felt from both himself and his team was a little overwhelming. So we delved into his hidden truth. We discovered an emotional backstory. He told us that he had always felt like he had less intellectual prowess than his peers. This had been drummed into him from an early age. During his birth, he had been slightly deprived of oxygen and his mother would tell anyone who would listen that "he's not that bright but he works hard to do his best". That conviction stayed with him and dictated his entire way of living and working. In order to keep up with his colleagues, he had made an unconscious pact with himself to work twice as hard as anyone else. Otherwise, he was unworthy of his position.

The moment that he articulated this hidden reality to his team, the situation in the company changed. Once they knew what had motivated him, his colleagues really understood him – which resulted in less stress. Now they perceived his feverish conduct as a dynamic to be avoided rather than emulated. The man himself was able to adapt his behaviour and to relax more. He asked the people around him to warn him if he relapsed into his old habits. As a result, it was as though a fresh wind were sweeping through the corridors. New energy was released; people related to him and to each other differently.

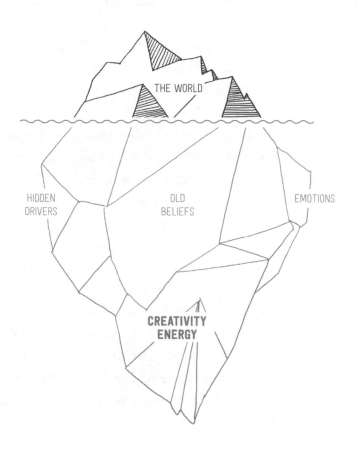

SOMETHING IS CHANGING

Nowadays, we are seeing an attempt to transcend the tendency to compartmentalise people in all sorts of spheres of life. We want to address our wider personal consciousness. It is as if we sense that we are missing out on something, that our lives and jobs could be richer if we could get beyond pigeonholing everyone.

For example, look at the phenomenon of self-organised teams, which is increasingly seen in organisations today. People are working without a supervisor and are making decisions about their own salaries, work commitments and holidays. By literally removing the compartments, they are forced to rely on their own sense of justice. This includes more emphasis on their experience and perception and less on the invisible mental framework. It is an example of how a change in structure can enable a more organic way of working whereby there is an explicit demand on employees to consciously put their skills to use.

> IT IS AS IF WE SENSE THAT WE ARE MISSING OUT ON SOMETHING, THAT OUR LIVES AND JOBS COULD BE RICHER IF WE COULD GET BEYOND PIGEONHOLING EVERYONE.

You can see it in the way we vote today. Voters shop around to find the candidate that appeals to them based on their personal experiences and impressions. This is a change from the tendency to stick within the confines of rational political reality. We vote more for people than for convictions or out of identification with a particular political party. Perhaps this is a signal that particracy is due for change. In science too, various fields are growing closer together. For example, in physics, specialists are penetrating so deeply into their knowledge of matter that their questions and solutions far exceed their own fields.

The point is to deploy all the different parts to make the whole better. When all the elements that we have stored untapped in our human reservoir are finally allowed to participate, then we will get more out of our lives and jobs. This is exactly what is happening now. We are slowly learning to balance our left brain with our right brain. Analytical distinctions remain important but are being complemented by what we experience, perceive, feel and sense.

WHEN ALL THE ELE-
MENTS THAT WE HAVE
STORED UNTAPPED IN
OUR HUMAN RESERVOIR
ARE FINALLY ALLOWED
TO PARTICIPATE, THEN
WE WILL GET MORE OUT
OF OUR LIVES AND JOBS.

Great changes are happening that are gradually transforming our world into one that is free of compartments. But if you really want to benefit from this you will have to overcome the compartments in yourself. The participative person starts by focusing on the forgotten parts of themselves. They can then participate in society in a fuller, clearer, more consistent and happier way. Every person deserves to be fully themselves in their lives. And to work in a company that employs the same dynamic to exploit the hidden powers of their employees.

It is important to develop tools that help people with this. Tools that also support companies and organisations in their endeavour to create a context that makes this possible. For one can also mine these hidden seams of energy in the workplace, resulting in every employee - and the company as a whole - feeling good and developing optimally. Even if the only outcome is that you notice more contented people in your company, colleagues who get far more from each other and themselves.

ONE CAN ALSO MINE THESE HIDDEN SEAMS OF ENERGY IN THE WORKPLACE, RESULTING IN EVERY EMPLOYEE - AND THE COMPANY AS A WHOLE - FEELING GOOD AND DEVELOPING OPTIMALLY.

In practice, we find that there are three easy steps to follow if you would like to make more of your own potential and that of your place of work:

FIND REAL INSPIRATION
PARTICIPATORY DRIVE

CONNECTEDNESS FOR CREATIVENESS
PARTICIPATORY CULTURE

CHARISMATIC ENGAGEMENT
PARTICIPATORY RESPONSIBILITY

In the following chapters, we will explore each of these steps in detail.

———

FIND REAL INSPIRATION
PARTICIPATORY DRIVE

OUR LIFE SCENARIO

Our society is overflowing with insights, ideas, tips and tricks to innovate and improve our lives. We live in extraordinary times in which yesterday's opportunities have already been superseded by those of today. Smartphones, an intelligent Internet, smart products, clothes that feel and cars that think: you name it, it exists. It sometimes seems as though we are in The Age of Magic, barely able to believe what we see happening around us.

Furthermore, every innovation and piece of news is instantly accessible. It turns the world into a global shopping street, where enticing products alternate in the blink of an eye with the most desperate suffering and horror. While technology offers new opportunities, it also disrupts the economy and society. And it just keeps flowing directly into our homes, day in, day out, at a dizzying rate that will not stop. This engenders a lot of pressure. And this pressure is amplified by successive financial crises, growing job insecurity and frequently volatile social and political situations in our own society.

It is striking that we allow this helter-skelter world to dominate our own lives, and thereby keep giving it oxygen. So not only do we play a lot of circumscribed roles, we also allow the scenario to be written for us by the outside world.

IT IS STRIKING THAT WE ALLOW THIS HELTER-SKELTER WORLD TO DOMINATE OUR OWN LIVES, AND THEREBY KEEP GIVING IT OXYGEN.

While one person might greedily absorb all the input and be afraid of missing something, another might shut themselves away and ban televisions or smartphones from their home. Both are expending a considerable amount of energy. The former by trying to control the overload, the latter by building a wall around their own life. Both are reacting to what is happening in a world that is not under their control.

Step into a subway train in any metropolis in the world at six or seven o'clock and you will see this dynamic in action.

A deep fatigue is evident in most of the faces, the stress almost palpable and certainly visible on many a yawning passenger. Reality rises to the surface from deep inside. At such times, the subway can feel like a twilight zone between the roles we play at work and the roles we play at home – the latter being where we can finally shrug off our burdens for a little while.

I sat, dead tired myself, on the Tokyo metro opposite two slumped men. One was a labourer, the other more of a banker type. Side by side, they were having an almost comatose nap together, practically holding each other up. I suddenly asked myself: What is driving us anyway? What is my inner inspiration? That I step into this world every day and attempt to control it, play the roles that I've become accustomed to and then return home like this? It was a question that would not let me go. Whereas this may have started as a passing thought, like the multitude of thoughts we have in any given day, after a while I started to take it seriously. And to really wonder: what is actually driving me to live like this?

I SUDDENLY ASKED MYSELF:
WHAT IS DRIVING US ANYWAY?
WHAT IS MY INNER INSPIRATION?
THAT I STEP INTO THIS WORLD EVERY
DAY AND ATTEMPT TO CONTROL IT,
PLAY THE ROLES THAT I'VE
BECOME ACCUSTOMED TO
AND THEN RETURN HOME LIKE THIS?

—

MASKS OFF

If we live and work as "divided" beings in a context that seems to be controlling our lives, then surely the first question we have to ask ourselves is: Who am I aside from the roles I play? Who is there behind all those compartments that dominate my daily life?

It is not easy to think about, let alone to answer, because the world is hurtling by at an unprecedented rate. It is so easy to lose ourselves in the insane impulses of each day - or to obstinately guard ourselves against the modern world - that there is little energy left to actually question our motives. Our focus is hostage to the outside world and barely ever trained on the inner world.

When you want to ask yourself what drives you, you have two options. You can look for the source of your drive in the outside world, the one in which you function: this might be a desire for success, money or respect. But you can also look within yourself for the motor that drives you: that's when it gets interesting. The answer will be far more profound. This is because you are now looking for your inner inspiration.

When you pose the question "What is my inner inspiration?", the focus changes. You gain an entirely different perspective on your life than you are used to. The spot to which we usually head for a view of our lives from a distance is somewhere above us. This fact is even ingrained in our vocabulary: we speak of looking at something from a helicopter perspective. What we do next is to stand on the tip of our iceberg and from there, survey ourselves and the busy world. What we see is solely the reality above the surface. It is a beautiful view, of course, and can often provide powerful insights.

But if you are wondering who you are and why you do what you do, you find a new vantage point from which to steer your life: the one underneath the iceberg. This is the place for a profound perspective. The view from there is larger and more contemplative since you do not only get a picture of the known reality but also of the unconscious and subconscious realities. It is also the place where your feelings get to be heard, where there is stillness and everything is completely unique to you. Because it is a perspective that is solely yours.

WHEN YOU POSE THE QUESTION "WHAT IS MY INNER INSPIRATION?", THE FOCUS CHANGES. YOU GAIN AN ENTIRELY DIFFERENT PERSPECTIVE ON YOUR LIFE THAN YOU ARE USED TO.

This is the place where you live without a mask, where you are in contact with your entire identity all at once, free from the many roles you assume. Here you are your real self and

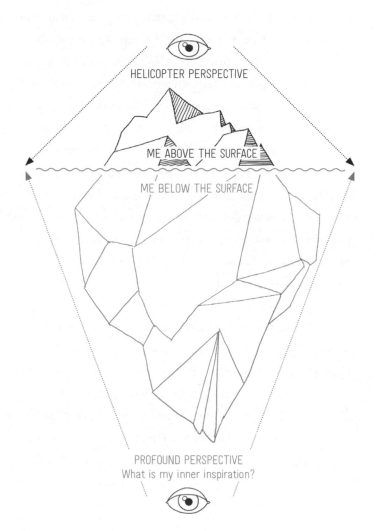

the way that you could choose to present yourself to the world above. You look at life differently because you are not seeing yourself in a category but as a whole. You are not identifying with just one side of yourself and you are not populating that part of yourself with the expectations of the world either. There are simply no expectations. This is the vantage point from which you can write your own scenario. You are 100 percent pure potential, detached from everything and yet more motivated than ever to live passionately. One could say that here you touch on a spiritual dimension of yourself, in the sense that you are searching for your deepest and most personal inner experience. This is what you use as a compass for who you are, what you do and how you connect with others and the world around you.

A useful metaphor that can help to visualise this place of profound insight is the moment of your birth. This is the moment when anything is possible. A moment when you have not yet taken on any role and do not yet really have a conscious ego. You are free of rational thought and experience the world as an organic whole. Emotion, perception, intuition and feelings are your drivers. You have barely had any stimulation, your mind is undeveloped, and, of course, you have not yet started

YOU ARE 100 PERCENT PURE POTENTIAL, DETACHED FROM EVERYTHING AND YET MORE MOTIVATED THAN EVER TO LIVE PASSIONATELY.

dividing up yourself or your world into separate pieces. Anything can happen.

It is the start of a journey during which your personality will be shaped by disparate experiences; you will be taught beliefs and truths; and, in the end, you will assume roles that you have been taught are yours. But just for a moment, before the journey has begun, you are free and uncompartmentalised. You are not a reductive version of yourself but 100 percent "I". All you can do from then on is to grow - to repeatedly attempt to overcome your limitations. There is a huge drive to do so. You could call it your inner inspiration. By invoking this power that exists deep inside you, you recreate the perspective that you need in order to be able to abandon your compartments.

———

ASK YOURSELF THE QUESTION You can expect a number of repercussions when you ask yourself about your inner inspiration. There are strings attached.

If you allow the question to really penetrate, you will feel an impact immediately. Ready to try?

The following visualisation exercise offers you a route into your inner inspiration: beyond the confines of the compartments in your life. One cannot predict how the exercise will impact on any one person. There are those who find it life-changing, who now look at the choices they make every day with greater clarity. There are others who do not feel anything or seem to get any insight from the exercise but who, a few days later, see their lives improve. And there are still others who do not really know what they are "supposed" to feel, or what they should do with the experience.

All reactions are perfectly fine. There is nothing that you should feel or experience. Whatever happens is dependant on the stage of your life that you are in, the roles that you are currently playing, the emotions that you feel right now and the choices that you have made up to this point. For this reason, you can do the exercise more than once. In fact, do it any time you feel stressed, have momentarily lost your way or would like to have a different perspective on yourself and your world.

The chances that it will have a real impact increase if you make a few prior agreements with yourself. These are agreements that allow your intuitive right-brain to be activated as well as your rational left-brain and make it more likely that the visualisation exercise will result in a response from deep within yourself:

1. Switch off your expectations
It is completely human when you start something to have a certain picture of what the outcome might be. But when you do, what you are actually doing is putting a piece of reality into a box before that reality even exists: into a box that suits your preconceptions. By switching off all conscious and unconscious expectations, you free up your ability to experience something. You can do this by simply telling yourself: "Whatever the outcome of this experience, it's fine by me".

2. Use all your senses
Be aware that you are more than just a thinker. That you can also receive information through your senses during this exercise. Some people will suddenly see images, hear

words or sounds, taste or smell something. Anything can happen. When you gain a vision of not just a part of yourself but of your whole being from a deeper perspective, all these channels are addressed. Take your time during the exercise to calmly observe everything that comes to you through your senses.

3. Surrender to your unconscious impulses

Know the feeling when something pops into your mind and then you immediately forget it? And then you ask yourself, what was it you wanted to say? (Followed by deciding that "it couldn't have been important".) It is precisely these intuitive impulses that you need to pay attention to and amplify. They are fleeting scraps of inspiration that your right-brain feeds to your mind. However absurd these passing thoughts may seem, pay attention without passing judgment.

ACCEPT THAT YOUR STREAM OF CONSCIOUSNESS WILL NOT STOP BUT DO NOT FOCUS ON IT. INSTEAD, CONCENTRATE ON THE EMPTY MOMENTS BETWEEN THOUGHTS.

During the exercise, quietly allow all your thoughts in but then immediately let them go. Accept that your stream of consciousness will not stop but do not focus on it. Instead, concentrate on the empty moments between thoughts. Try to pick up what your mind is telling you. Keep it playful so that you do not become frustrated.

VISUALISATION EXERCISE: WHAT IS MY INNER INSPIRATION?

30 min

There are several ways to perform this exercise. You can read it through first, memorise it and then do the exercise step by step; you can ask someone else to read it out loud to you; or you can record the text and then play it back while you perform the exercise. You can also find an audio text at **yourworkandyourlife.com.**

The first step is aimed at relaxation and allows you to focus on yourself. In the second step, we activate the imagination. Take your time with these first steps. The more intensely you experience them, the more powerful the later experience.

Make sure that you have half an hour to yourself. Find a place where you feel comfortable and where you will not be disturbed. Switch off your mobile phone and any other potentially disturbing sources of noise in the space. Sit in a comfortable chair or, for example, cross-legged on a cushion. It is better to close your eyes during this exercise. This helps you to direct your attention inwards.

Step 1: **Be aware**

Take a moment to make sure you are sitting properly and feel comfortable. Relax and become aware of your body, of how you are sitting.

Now focus on your feet. Notice how they feel. Are they heavy, light, flexible, energetic or rather tired? Feel your toes, your soles, your heels, your calves. Simply experience the sensations that come to you. Experience them without feeling that you need to form thoughts. If thoughts intrude, allow them in but then immediately let them go again. See them as a river that's passing by. Let your attention move slowly higher, to your shins, your knees and thighs. What do you notice? What are the sensations that go with it? Whatever you feel, register it, observe it. Any feeling you have is perfectly fine. Relax, observe, let go and move on.

Gently climb upwards. Observe how you are sitting and how your body is touching the chair or the cushion. How does it feel? Move to your belly, your chest and back. What do you experience in this region? Do you have a tense or relaxed stomach, can you feel your heart beating, is your back burdened or unburdened? Explore these zones bit by bit. Experience how all the parts of this "system" feel. Repeatedly allow your stream of consciousness to simply flow by. Receive your thoughts and let them go.

Finally, travel all the way up and focus on your throat, neck, face and the crown of your head. What do you feel there? Is there a zone that demands your attention, stands out or signals to you? Zoom in and submit to the experience. Do this in a calm and relaxed way.

Step 2: **Let go**
Focus on your breathing. Feel how you breathe in the air and then breathe it out. Take your time to observe the rhythm of your breathing. Continue until you notice that your rhythm of inhaling and exhaling has become soft and gentle.

Now recall the parts of your body where you sensed tension. Shift your attention to them and breathe in deeply, as though you were inhaling the tension. Then release it in a long exhalation. Sigh away the stress from every zone in your body that asks for attention. Consciously keep the rhythm of your breathing slow. Maintain the cadence of your breath.

Remain calmly present in your experience. Cherish your space as you calmly breathe in and out.

Step 3: Activate your imagination and open your senses

Imagine that you have just been born. You have barely been in the world and are at the beginning of your journey. You are utterly yourself and everything is still possible. You have not yet made any choices, you do not yet think rationally or in terms of compartments. Your right-brain is totally free and pushes you - the intuitive creature full of imagination and potential - forward. You look at the life ahead of you without any idea of what it will be. Anything can happen, you can still go in any direction.

Use all your senses to experience how this feels: if you are a visual person, then focus on the images you see in your mind's eye; if you are more a sensual person, experience what is happening in your body. You may hear words or taste things. Notice the way that you are experiencing things. Dive right into the sensation. Make it your own. Feel the pure potential, the incredible range of possibilities and inspirations that lie ahead of you. Most importantly, make contact with the spark of passion that is there in you.

Step 4: The question

Look at what happens when you make contact with this spark. And pose the question below to the intuitive being that you are. You can say it out loud to increase its impact.

**What is the inspiration and passion
that drives my life?**

Go ahead and repeat the question two or three times. Feel the impact of the words on your system. Focus on the silences and pauses between the thoughts that still arrive automatically. Do that for a while. Take the time to experience the stillness.

Step 5: **The answer**

Use all your senses once more to intercept the answer that emerges from the deeper perspective of where you are now. Keep focusing on the spaces between your thoughts. See, experience, hear, smell or taste whatever surfaces. The answer may come to you in an unexpected way. Just register what happens. If an emotion emerges, that's fine. Give it space and observe it. Allow whatever happens to happen and rest a while in this place of calm epiphany.

Step 6: **Finish**

If you sense that the visualisation is coming to an end, make a point of saying goodbye to this part of your space that you have now explored. This makes it easier and faster to return to later. Concentrate on your body again. Be aware of your breathing and of all your limbs. You can squeeze your hands together so that you gently "awaken". Become aware of your surroundings again and slowly open your eyes.

Step 7: **Process**

Keep to yourself a little longer, with your eyes open.

Don't immediately share your experiences with anyone. Try to hold on to what you experienced long enough to put it down on paper. Make an effort to address the following questions:

- What have I experienced or seen and what emotions did this arouse? (Describe it in your own words, as concretely as possible.)
- What part of it was new or surprising to me?
- What insight does this give me into the life I now lead?

By articulating your experience, you open up a way for new information to enter your consciousness. But you can also draw or visualise it: whatever feels most comfortable to you. You have pulled out pieces of yourself from the deeper perspective that are now being introduced into your "system".

For the next few days, pay attention to what has changed in your mind, your body and your behaviour. Try to recall this experience regularly in the week that follows. Observe how you react and how your insight into yourself, and the theme that emerges, grows. This deepens the experience.

As soon as you are able to express clearly what happened to you, share it with family, friends or colleagues whom you trust and with whom you feel safe. This is the final step to bringing your subconscious into the light of day. It generally stirs up strong reactions, which only serve to confirm your feelings.

Your experience of this exercise does not necessarily have to be "nice" or "good". It may even be that you stumble on a part of yourself that you subconsciously suppressed because you didn't like it. But you release new energy by giving that part of yourself space as well.

A man who tried this visualisation said afterwards that the exercise was a total failure. He had experienced and seen a lot, but the experience itself was not positive. He had managed to relax and to open up his imagination and senses. But when he asked himself the question and focused on the space between his thoughts, he felt trapped in a small, dark, damp and depressing place. His consciousness clung on to that for the entire duration of the exercise.

His question as to what he should do with that image was pertinent. It appeared that his deeper perspective was a gloomy place and one that he did not want to be in. How could space and energy be drawn from such a source?

WHEN HE ASKED HIMSELF THE QUESTION AND FOCUSED ON THE SPACE BETWEEN HIS THOUGHTS, HE FELT TRAPPED IN A SMALL, DARK, DAMP AND DEPRESSING PLACE.

This experience was not, in fact, a failure. Even though it was unpleasant, information had been retrieved.

The man deliberately replayed this image and the accompanying feelings every day for a week. This changed his perspective. He slowly realised that he was not giving himself the space to live and that this came from a deep-rooted conviction that he didn't deserve to exist. 'It's true', he said, 'that I really don't give myself much space. I'm always there for others, always looking for company, inviting friends to my home every weekend to avoid being alone. But basically that's exhausting. Maybe I have to revisit that dark cellar in myself in order to calmly figure out how I can enlarge that space.'

This insight brought a certain amount of emotions and grief to the surface but also relief. The man explained how he only realised now that he had lived with a great deal of tension caused by not wanting to be alone. That tension had diminished and become more manageable due to the deeper perspective that he had found.

CALM

The first thing that many people notice when they "ask the crucial question" is a sense of calm. And that a lot of the background noise of life disappears. As if they are suddenly sharply aware of what is truly important and what is not. It is as if they have set in motion a PPS: a personal positioning system. You see all the stimuli in your life but you are more able to disentangle the main issues from the secondary ones. Your priorities become clearer. The over-stimulating world is still there, of course, and you don't fight it but, having asked this question of yourself, you seem to be more aware of what is or is not important.

Everything regulates itself without the need for you to compartmentalise: things just fall into place. You notice a sort of organic order that allows you to distinguish more readily between main and side issues. It seems easier to make new decisions that will help you to move forward. In other words, a profound perspective brings a sense of calm with it that enables you to evolve from an intellectual structure that you control to one that is more organic, natural and effortless. This form of order has always existed: by looking at the world differently and with more detachment, it will become perceptible to you.

> YOU NOTICE A SORT OF ORGANIC ORDER THAT ALLOWS YOU TO DISTINGUISH MORE READILY BETWEEN MAIN AND SIDE ISSUES.

THE LANGUAGE OF FEELING

Another interesting result of posing this question is that it is clear that there is no instant, concrete answer to it. This can be experienced as frustration, since our left hemisphere wants specific, concrete answers. But if you look beyond this and free the words of these shackles, then you will notice how your thoughts will be accompanied by new feelings, experiences and emotions. That makes sense because this is a question that shakes you out of the compartments in your left brain and opens the door to a broader perspective that pays more heed to your unconscious feelings. Your reality under the table, so to speak.

> IF YOU LOOK BEYOND THIS AND FREE THE WORDS OF THESE SHACKLES, THEN YOU WILL NOTICE HOW YOUR THOUGHTS WILL BE ACCOMPANIED BY NEW FEELINGS, EXPERIENCES AND EMOTIONS.

SHADOWS

When you look at the world from a vantage point that includes your unconscious reality, then you inevitably encounter a darker side of yourself. You meet old fears that you have always repressed so that you could just get on with life and deep convictions that you have always pushed into the same old compartment. These are all aspects of yourself in which you have actually invested a lot of energy. So there you are rooting around in your shadowy, subconscious energy reserve. This is, of course, the intention. You want to bring the power that is stored there up to the surface of your life.

The actor we met up with told us that she had been trapped in the "serious actor" compartment for quite a while. She described this social category as a culture in which you're only accepted if you do "heavy" intellectual theatre work, avoid TV parts, turn down presentation jobs in the corporate world and certainly refuse to act in a soap. She was terrified that her credibility would be affected, that she would no longer be offered "real jobs" if she failed to honour these prescripts. But when she addressed her deeper perspective, she felt that she would actually love to explore these other worlds. She wanted to make full use of her creativity.

But there was something inside of her that had long kept her from doing this. It seemed to be a deep-seated fear of being rejected, of not belonging. As a child, she was sometimes shut out of the group of friends that she wanted to be a part of and bullied for being "different". By dealing with the fear and simply experiencing the emotions that went with it, she found the strength in herself to take a different path. Space was now available for the side of herself that wanted to act in a commercial play or on TV. She decided to follow her heart and let go of all her old beliefs.

These days, she alternates with great delight between serious plays, comedies and TV series. She feels much better and doesn't have the impression that anyone is judging her for her choices. Or perhaps she simply doesn't notice. Physically, she is also in a better, more relaxed place. The tension that she felt in her shoulders has disappeared.

—

THE KEY: ALLOW EMOTIONS

If we deal with these types of subconscious obstacles instead of suppressing them, then we save a lot of energy. With the new sense of freedom and self-awareness that we gain from this energy, we can explore and experiment with new opportunities in our lives.

It is essential that we do not habitually suppress the emotions that we encounter. The outside world is rational, the inside world is emotional. When you learn to notice your own feelings and to accept and really experience them rather than trying to avoid them, you are creating a new energy platform. Whether it is sadness, fear or anger, if you consciously accept and experience what you feel, then these emotions fade away. When someone goes through this, they often become suddenly aware of the origin of a stubborn emotion or belief. At that moment, they have excavated their unconscious or subconscious.

I had the idea to write a book about my experiences working with people and companies but it was many months before I actually did anything about it. Every day, I found myself sucked into my usual routine. I would work my way through as many files as I could at great speed day in and day out. And I was only just keeping up, so it appeared to be necessary. I couldn't escape for a second. My schedule was overflowing with meetings, coaching sessions and lectures. The book idea was becoming a sword of Damocles hanging over my head - an increasingly menacing shadow. It was one job that I wasn't getting done.

Until I asked myself what in God's name was motivating me and then withdrew momentarily to experience what this question aroused in me. When I looked for my inner inspiration, the first thing I felt was sadness. Sadness about the lost opportunity it would be if I didn't write the book. The missed chance to share my ideas with those who might have been interested. Whenever I had shared, I had the feeling that I was contributing something meaningful. It was part of my reason for existence. I would feel better and more energetic.

As soon as I allowed in and absorbed the sadness, it was as if my reality once again rearranged itself. This book became a priority. It had to exist. I would be doing myself an injustice if I ignored it any more. This feeling gave me the energy and passion to begin. Fears still crept in, such as the conviction that the company couldn't function without me ("If I take the time off to write, then our business will go down the drain"). But once I acknowledged them, they ebbed away.

I was relieved that when I told my colleagues, they found it natural. When I explained what exactly I wanted to document, an exciting energy was released that really drove me on. At the time of writing this, I note that the work on this book and even my absence from the office have served to breathe new life into everyone.

It may well be that underneath one emotion lies another one buried. Do not be discouraged by this. Try to simply experience and accept it each time.

Your body is a true bellwether of whether you are tapping into your subconscious. When you are confronted with an unprocessed emotion, it often manifests as something physical. You start to sweat, feel it in your stomach or guts, or maybe as an actual pain in your neck. Our bodies are accurate barometers that tell us when we are dealing with a shadow and therefore a hidden energy reserve.

—

THE PARTICIPATORY DRIVE

When you convert an unconscious driver into a conscious one, then you experience a new passion that gives your life direction and clarity. You are mining prodigious energy stores that can now be consciously deployed in your life. We call this participatory drive. By allowing the unconscious parts of yourself to participate, you are empowering yourself. This is how we generate fresh inspiration and creativity.

This is an energy source that you can return to time and again to feel more fully human. The more you return to this well, the more opportunities you create for yourself in the world around you and the more sense you give your own life. It is like a spiral or DNA strand that takes you inwards, each twist and turn leading to a more deeply felt level. The harder you hunt for your inner inspiration, the more you move along the path to self-transcendence.

People sometimes approach me after a lecture to congratulate me on its content but hasten to add that the insights "only apply to the happy few". And that, while *they* understand what it is all about, one cannot expect a labourer or factory worker to ask themselves what the meaning of their life is. This is a way of thinking that I cannot agree with.

Obviously these are questions that have value for every human being, whether they work behind a cash register or in some creative profession. Actually, we find that people who have a less intellectually strenuous job demonstrate fewer inhibitions about discussing their lives from the deeper perspective.

———

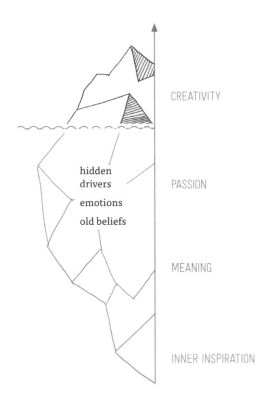

INSPIRED COMPANIES

The same dynamics can be applied at the organisational level. After all, people who work together operate from shared principles. Organisations, like people, are a "system" of actions and reactions. Every day, we work with others in what can potentially become a straitjacket of automatism. It pays to have the courage to ask a tricky question: Why do you work together? And what is the driving force behind what you want to achieve as a whole?

When you pose these questions as a company, you start the journey to your deeper organisational perspective. And are better able to identify why you do what you do together, day in and day out. Providing clarity about this gives employees certainty and peace of mind. It also offers people a reference point for their own deeper desires. This is, of course, first and foremost a job for management, which is responsible for formulating the common goal or vision.

If you would like to establish a common drive of this sort, then it is useful to go back into the past, to the moment that the company was founded. By looking at the founders' original vision for the company, you return to the birth of the structure. And you ask yourself what remains of it and how you can apply the initial spirit to today's reality. At the same time, this can be very confrontational. You may find yourself coming across unresolved sensitivities from the past that have become rooted in the corporate culture.

The quest for the "soul" of your company also generates answers that go beyond simple strategic goals. You arrive at formulations that establish a dream that transcends daily work. This is precisely what arouses the passions of people.

Years ago, a shoe retailer asked us to help them find new impetus. The CEO literally said: 'We need fresh oxygen in the company to get us through the next ten years.' Management members went through a number of soul-searching sessions, which included a look back at the time when an earlier generation of the family started the chain store. They also asked themselves about the company's current inspiration and motivation. It was a particularly engrossing – and also affecting – two days that exposed a number of old convictions and emotions that had lodged themselves in the corporate culture.

They went through an intensive process that enabled the company to completely revise its purpose. Now it reads: "360° considerateness leads to 360° profit". There is no more talk of shoes but instead of caring for each other. The company developed a work culture based on real interpersonal contact,

commitment and connectivity. And one that considers profit
not only in terms of financial growth but also as the personal
well-being and happiness of the employees. With great open-
ness and conviction, management does its best every single
day to make this happen. And it shows in the retailer's new
energy. The chain's image is improving year by year, along
with its sales figures. This is unsurprising since there is now
a common drive that is powered and shared by the employees.
And that is immediately recognised by customers.

When an organisation is clear about its driving force, then it becomes much easier for an employee to see whether or not they fit in. In other words, if their personal passion matches the employer's company culture. Any group of employees can reflect on the meaning or lack of meaning in their job when a company is unequivocal. For example, they can ask themselves questions such as "What motivated us to work for this company?" "What made us want to work for the government?" "Why do we do what we do together?" "Are we all stuck in rigid systems of collaboration?" "What are the behaviour patterns that prevent us from doing our jobs with more appetite and passion?" These are all relevant questions that should be addressed in all work

IN A PERSONAL PRO-
CESS, YOUR BODY IS A
RELIABLE BAROMETER
OF HOW COMFORTABLE
OR UNCOMFORTABLE YOU
FEEL WHEN YOU TAP
INTO AN UNFAMILIAR
VEIN OF ENERGY. IN A
GROUP IT IS HUMOUR.

environments so that you can get the best out of yourself and each other. This is how you overturn the seemingly insurmountable and at times emotional obstacles with which you will certainly be confronted.

In a personal process, your body is a reliable barometer of how comfortable or uncomfortable you feel when you tap into an unfamiliar vein of energy. In a group it is humour. Again and again, it can be observed that when underlying emotions are touched on, the group deals with feelings of discomfort by becoming noisier and telling sarcastic jokes. For coaches, remarks such as "Okay, let's just let all our feelings hang out!" or "I really don't need to know how much you like me, you know" are signs that they are doing something right. Indeed, these are perfectly natural reactions that usually lighten up a situation.

——

ANOTHER WAY TO LOOK AT MONEY

In practice, one often sees growth arrive in the form of a change in attitude to money. No matter how you look at it, the truth is that money is now the driving force in all levels of our society. This is, at face value, logical. We live in an acutely rational context. And when you rationalise reality, you end up with numbers. The way that society makes figures tangible is through money. This has become the foundation and the yardstick for our work and our lives.

But when you delve deeper in search of your inner inspiration, you automatically change your relationship with money. It is not that it becomes insignificant but rather that its significance is now as a means to an end. Your perspective on your life broadens while money shrinks to just one aspect of it. It always comes back to the wider human factor. That factor is not limited to a rational profit maximisation but instead accounts for the welfare and well-being of people, both employees and clients. From the moment we address and expose the non-rational part of ourselves, we relativise the quantified world.

> WHEN YOU DELVE DEEPER IN SEARCH OF YOUR INNER INSPIRATION, YOU AUTOMATICALLY CHANGE YOUR RELATIONSHIP WITH MONEY. IT IS NOT THAT IT BECOMES INSIGNIFICANT BUT RATHER THAT ITS SIGNIFICANCE IS NOW AS A MEANS TO AN END.

This movement cuts our materialistic way of thinking down to size. Perhaps economics can return to being the true human science that it should be. Economics is essentially intended as a means to enable the fair exchange of value(s) between people. It should not be about the maximisation of the profit for one at the expense of the other.

> *There are a considerable number of people and companies these days that are experimenting with or employing the participatory business model. And then there are those who just think they are. We encounter them in our work sometimes. So we met this entrepreneur, who said to us: 'Inner inspiration? Drive? Passion? Creativity? Yep, all present and accounted for. I feel inspired to create value. That's where my passion to make as much money as I can comes from. I'm very creative in that way. I always find another means to create more sales and more profit.'*

> *To be fair, he said all this with a slightly challenging smile. But he was using the precepts of the participatory company to justify his unerringly rational mindset and to avoid thinking about his own underlying reality. We actually call this "disengaged drive" as opposed to "participatory drive".*

> *It was good to see how prepared the man was - out of a healthy curiosity - to dig a little deeper into himself. It turned*

out that he had grown up in a very poor family and had lost both his parents young. His father had managed to support them but, as a labourer, had completely worn out his body. As a kid, the entrepreneur had convinced himself that it was his fault. And he needed to compensate for this by making ever more money. The drawback was that he barely saw his own children and had experienced two health warnings. The realisation that he was taking the same route as his late father brought up a lot of raw emotion. His view of life changed drastically, as did his actual life and that of his family.

—

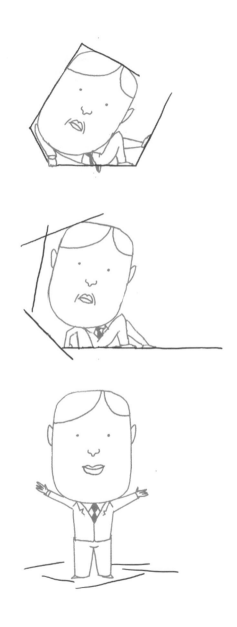

CONNECTEDNESS FOR CREATIVENESS
PARTICIPATORY CULTURE

FROM EGO TO WE-GO

Participatory drive may seem a little selfish at first glance. It seems to require detaching yourself from the world in which you live. You might also think that this entails disassociating yourself and closing yourself off from your environment. Surely the intention cannot be to create a world in which everyone is turned inwards, constantly focusing on their own reality?

Fortunately, this is not what happens in practice. The individual or organisation that searches for its own participatory drive experiences a very interesting paradox. Those who delve into their deeper selves in a sincere attempt to find their inner inspiration notice that they actually become more aware of their roles in their community and society as a whole. This makes sense. When one integrates a forgotten part of oneself, one feels more fully engaged with one's world. As a result, relationships will also subtly change.

The part of ourselves that tries to keep daily life above the waterline of our iceberg could be considered to be our ego. It appears to be attached to the compartments that it uses to try to control the outside world and also disengaged from its own deeper being. In fact, it never establishes real relationships or attachments above the surface.

The first thing that happens when you search for your inner inspiration is that forgotten parts of yourself become reintegrated into your consciousness. You become "more yourself". This allows your surface ego to feel like a more essential part of the world. You transcend the compartments that you trapped yourself in until now. And that changes your entire outlook on the world. You begin to see everything and everyone around you as equal to you, instead of as opponents who come from a different compartment. These are allies with whom you

YOU BEGIN TO SEE EVERYTHING AND EVERYONE AROUND YOU AS EQUAL TO YOU, INSTEAD OF AS OPPONENTS WHO COME FROM A DIFFERENT COMPARTMENT. THESE ARE ALLIES WITH WHOM YOU CAN WORK SIDE BY SIDE TO BUILD A BETTER, HAPPIER AND MORE NOURISHING LIFE.

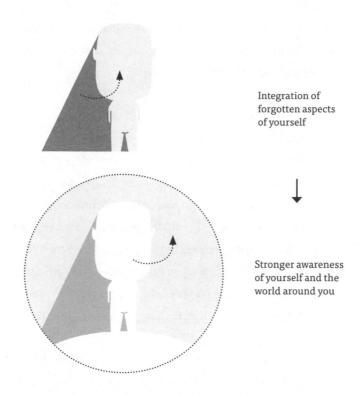

Integration of
forgotten aspects
of yourself

↓

Stronger awareness
of yourself and the
world around you

can work side by side to build a better, happier and more nourishing life. Your connections quickly evolve into balanced relationships where you create more value for each other.

We note that people who seek their inner inspiration invariably develop greater self-awareness and a clearer, more empathetic and nuanced view of the world. They open up a new perspective that gives their lives more substance and colour and the people around them more meaning. In other words, they have found a firmer mooring from which to consciously identify and connect with the world.

A highly talented editor devoted most of his time to guiding writers and editing their work. Not only was he a phenomenal wordsmith but also an extremely astute judge of character. He would instantly grasp how a writer functioned, what their sensitivities were and how to identify the nuances and passion in their work. For fifteen years, this made him an invisible but indispensable pillar of the writing community, and one who liked to work in the privacy of his own home. Everyone in his circle had been encouraging him for years to write his own book. But something was holding him back.

When he learned about the participatory principle, he was very enthusiastic to try the soul-searching exercise. A powerful emotion surfaced as he revisited his childhood and realised that he had not been given much space to have his own voice. He had always had to fight for his rightful place among his siblings. As the youngest of the pack, he was always "our baby" and no one really listened to him.

Once he had allowed in the emotions that accompanied this memory, his feelings and his situation underwent a dramatic change. He felt a new, instinctive self-assurance that made him decide to start writing. One day after the exercise, he began his first book. One week after that, he announced that to his amazement he had even more to report: so many new things were happening in both his professional and private life. 'It's as if I'm sending out a new, more inviting signal to the world,' he explained, 'unconsciously giving the impression that you're very welcome to come and see me and I won't bite if you come into my "lair".'

His story is a great example of how your relationship with the world is fundamentally strengthened when you dive below your own surface. The writer integrated a forgotten part of himself and therefore felt like a more complete participant in the world in which he lived. This was shown by the fact that he wanted to share his knowledge and talent more explicitly, in the hope that whosoever read his work would extract some value from it.

In fact, here we can see that a deeper personal awareness is the nucleus of an increasingly mature world consciousness. This is the essence of the participatory dynamic that one becomes aware of and experiences. The more completely you can be yourself, the more fully and consciously you participate in the world. The more you invest in yourself, the more you identify with all living beings. This is a critical insight into human development: as your individuality becomes

THE MORE COMPLETELY YOU
CAN BE YOURSELF, THE MORE
FULLY AND CONSCIOUSLY YOU
PARTICIPATE IN THE WORLD.
AS YOUR INDIVIDUALITY
BECOMES MORE PROFOUND,
YOU EXPERIENCE YOURSELF
AS A TOUCHINGLY UNIQUE
PART OF ALL THAT EXISTS.

more profound, you experience yourself as a touchingly unique part of all that exists.

WHAT IF...

You can also use this "global perspective" to find or specify the participatory drive or inner inspiration of a team. This can be achieved through a simple brainstorming exercise. It's best to start with groups of four or five people and then share all the acquired insights in the larger group.

Start from the idea that you're all stepping into a dream together. Take some time imagining that together you can experience and change everything that's happening in the world. Anything is possible: you can bring in anything you want, wherever and however you want it. Because you simply are the world. Try to experience how this feels. Then ask the following question: How would you describe yourself as a world? What would you do, what would you change, what would you create with the talents that you have?

If one asks oneself this question and allows oneself or one's team to approach it as creatively as possible for an hour or two, it can result in often surprising and passionate drivers being addressed. The starting point of the exercise is the outside world, which is easier to employ as a reference point in the rational context of life as we know it today. But by making it our own, we instinctively draw on the deeper perspectives within ourselves.

You do not have to think in terms of limitations to define yourself. But you will not lose sight of yourself in the process. When, step by step, you integrate the world with yourself, the act of discovering who you are and where you want to go is faster and more intensive.

And that makes sense: the more you regard this planet and all that happens on it as a part of yourself, the more inspiration you will find time and again to progress in your life and work. The more you will find yourself surpassing your own expectations. And above all, the more enthusiasm and passionate commitment you will put into everything you do. Participatory thinking is underpinned by modern global self-awareness. After all, we are no longer looking for ourselves in the world. We are seeking the world in ourselves. And when you find that, the burden of carrying it simply slips away...

The waves of nationalism that regularly engulf countries are a good example. People tend to retreat into themselves and close their borders when they feel that their own prosperity is threatened. When this sort of movement leads to a process whereby a people returns to its roots, examines past traumas and tries to resolve them, then an awareness of our common humanity can develop that actually leads to unity between different countries. A heightened sense of your own identity doesn't have to mean that you give up your faith in the world. On the contrary, it demonstrates that you think it's worth the effort to share the best of yourself with the world. However, nationalist movements often forget this and get caught up in promulgating an image of the enemy that is usually no more than a reflection of their own trauma.

A HEIGHTENED SENSE OF YOUR OWN IDENTITY DOESN'T HAVE TO MEAN THAT YOU GIVE UP YOUR FAITH IN THE WORLD.

———

A SIMPLE PRINCIPLE

Once you experience yourself as a meaningful part of the world, you instantly see that it is pointless to only pursue profits for yourself. It becomes clear that you have to care for your environment and the wider world if you are to look after yourself. You discover that your sense of well-being and happiness only increases when you make sure that in everything you do it is not only you but also your immediate surroundings - and by extension the entire world - that benefits.

Our world could be changed for good by what is actually a very simple rule of thumb, a basic principle for living and working together. We call it the "ME-WE principle". It works like this: I am an integral part of the whole. Therefore I strive so that I, my environment and the rest of the world may profit from everything I do.

When we use this intention to evolve from ego to "we-go", our greater self-awareness creates a deep engagement with every living thing. I regard this as a fundamental principle that any human being from any background can make the effort to apply more consciously. The principle can be combined with any existing mental organisational models, leadership systems or personal development methods that may be useful.

THE
**ME
WE**
PRINCIPLE

I AM AN INTEGRAL PART OF THE WHOLE.
THEREFORE I STRIVE SO THAT I,
MY ENVIRONMENT AND THE REST OF THE WORLD
MAY PROFIT FROM EVERYTHING I DO.

The ME-WE principle is like an extra dimension that you add on in the knowledge that there is no barrier between you and the world around you. And that you benefit, therefore, when what you do benefits your environment. This is essentially the basic principle of economics, where each party in a relationship must be able to retain an equal stake in the results of the common effort.

The left hemisphere of your brain may protest a little at this. For example, an understandable reaction could be: "Everything you do must be for the good of the whole world as well as yourself? Isn't that impossible? There would be nothing left that we could do. You can't be expected to do everything for the good of others?"

Of course not. That's why it is a principle and not a law or regulation. Rules and regulations make coexistence possible by establishing where our personal space ends and the community begins. We need these laws to live in a more or less orderly society. But you cannot make the ME-WE principle enforceable. It does not fall within the remit of organising society according to compartments. Instead, it is an appeal to your sense of purpose as a human being. It is an endeavour

IT IS AN ENDEAVOUR THAT MAKES IT WORTH GETTING OUT OF BED EVERY DAY. YOU DO NOT EVEN NEED TO HAVE INORDINATE IDEALS: YOU COULD TRY IT JUST BE- CAUSE IT FEELS GOOD.

that makes it worth getting out of bed every day. You do not even need to have inordinate ideals: you could try it just because it feels good.

From the moment you apply this participatory drive principle, you will feel better and more balanced. And slowly but surely, you will get more back from the world around you in the form of appreciation, new insights or financial gain. The more complete and authentic a person you prove yourself to be, the stronger the response that "naturally" arises. Call it a positive boomerang: one that is worth more every time it returns.

A good way to preserve a balance between ME and WE is to employ "expectation management". Try to apply the ME-WE principle without attaching specific expectations to it, such as "This will earn me more money" or "Now my arch enemy at work will treat me differently". Such expectations will just put you back in a compartment, one that is dependent on the collusion of the outside world to make your personal aspirations and dreams come true. When you let go of expectations, it is easier to handle any negative reactions. After all, you cannot demand that the whole world instantly joins in with your ME-WE narrative. And it does not have to. Furthermore, you will then have more energy for the nourishing input that also comes your way.

A manager in a government organisation explained that the outside world was constantly damaging her. She spoke particularly of her predecessor. He had been transferred to a different function but still managed to undermine her repeatedly. 'I keep thinking that he is going to be friendly, open and constructive when a proposal of mine has to pass by him, but each time he is blunt, rude and always looks for my weaknesses. You are trying to apply a principle whereby everyone benefits in such a situation. I'd rather punch him in the face.'

The manager agreed to try to let go of her expectations about reactions when she submitted a proposal. Especially when it concerned her predecessor. From now on, she would only observe what happened and what sort of energy she was emitting. The result was that, as she put it, she could relativise and pay less attention to "the whining of her tormentor". In addition, when drafting a proposal she found herself far more detached and clear-sighted about what she thought was best for everyone than she had been before. This also meant that she could articulate her ideas better. Finally, she felt that she had more space to deal with the nuanced reactions she received and to benefit from them.

MANUAL FOR CHANGE

Your view of the world changes when you use the ME-WE principle as a guide in your life. The way that you perceive the people and situations that you encounter alters. You find yourself instinctively exploring actions and reactions that will either strengthen or weaken you and your environment. In other words, you are much more present in the world. And you find that you build relationships that are different to how they were before: deeper, more satisfying and helpful in illuminating new dimensions of yourself.

Imagine if we all tried to live according to this principle: the world would be a better place. For everyone.

This principle can be extended to cover all sorts of areas of life, whether personal or in companies and organisations. Sales training for shop sales teams is a good illustration of this. The traditional approach is to coach staff in ways to increase sales and, more specifically, sell extra services alongside the products. However, these days it is of more interest to avoid coaching that is only aimed at greater profits and instead focus on the following question from the perspective of the ME-WE principle: "How can I develop a durable and honest win-win relationship with each customer?".

So with this in mind, we set to work with a retail chain. We practised communication methods focused on real and genuine interactions with people, on listening properly and on giving honest advice. We received incredibly positive feedback from the sales team. The mood was one of stress and submissiveness at the start but it evolved to become one of enthusiasm to see the principle put into practice in the shops. The salesperson who invests in real concern for their customers experiences far more satisfaction in their life and work. A lasting relationship with the customer is forged, meaning that they will be back. And so long as that continues, the salesperson will not be out of pocket.

In the years to come, the greatest innovations will grow from this principle. This can already be seen in the sharing economy (where networks of people from all over the world trade directly with each other or develop products together without the middleman of an organisation or company), and, for example, in the contemporary interpretation of the cooperative system (in which the ownership of companies is in the hands of the employees and/or customers, and decisions are made based on ethical values).

OTHER NEW WAYS OF LIVING AND WORKING TOGETHER WILL BE CREATED, FOR WHICH LEGAL FRAMEWORKS HAVE NOT YET BEEN IMPOSED.

Other new ways of living and working together will be created, for which legal frameworks have not yet been imposed. This makes sense: a legal framework is based on compartments, while the ME-WE principle transcends them. An example of this is the alternative taxi service Uber, whose business concept and service in its early days fell outside of all sorts of legal frameworks and presented many governments with a headache.

We are at a turning point today, with so many diverse initiatives that seek to overturn our former structures. And many innovative ideas start out from a principle of value for everyone but soon turn into nothing more than new avenues for generating cash. Before they know it, they have relapsed into old ways of thinking and acting – perhaps because they lack the role models to do otherwise. So we are also in a transitional phase between a purely rational system and a much more balanced economic model. This involves trial and error.

——

THE CHALLENGE

The ME-WE principle can serve as a catalyst for lasting change. The following is a fun brainstorming exercise that you can do in a group. It is recommended to set aside a few hours for this.

Divide into groups of four or five people. It is usually better not to create teams of people who work together every day but instead to select people from different departments. The cross-pollination of ideas is usually much stronger and there will be less temptation to fall back into the usual patterns of working relationships.

Step 1: **Relaxation and activating the right-brain**
Move the group away from its comfort zone. For example, play some pulsating music and invite the participants to go wild. This is a safe and relaxed way for people to step out of their collective, rational mindset. It is not compulsory but can be helpful.

Step 2: **Associative responses**
Give everyone a pile of post-its and the assignment to complete the sentences – rapidly and intuitively – that

you will read out. They should write down the first thing that comes to mind and stop when they have nothing more to say. One response per post-it. The sentences are as follows:

- In my life, I need...
- My colleagues need...
- Our customers and the entire world needs...

Step 3: **Sharing in small groups**

Ask the participants in each group to briefly share their responses with each other and thereby impart what they think they, their environment and the world needs. During this step, it is only important that they listen to each other and create an understanding of each other's perspectives.

Step 4: **The challenge**

Now ask each group the following question:
"If we were to pursue profit for ourselves, each other, our customers and the whole of society in everything we do:

- What would we need to change in our organisation?
- And what would the outcome be?"

Give each group the assignment to devise a concept plan, including the first concrete step towards its implementation. The plan should be one that everyone can both identify with and see how the ME-WE principle is applied. It is important that participants can perceive the added value for themselves. Make sure that everyone gets to have a say. Ask that people consciously make space for each other. All groups will be expected to present their ideas. The method of doing so is up to them.

Step 5: The presentations
Each group gives a short but powerful presentation of their ME-WE plan and the first concrete step that they wish to take. Optional: organise a vote to filter for the best ME-WE ideas.

This is a fairly simple exercise that often results in highly original ideas. But the main focus is on training the ME-WE reflex, whereby people start to see how added value for themselves also implies added value for those around them. And vice versa.

A MATTER OF TIME

Can we succeed using only this one principle? Is it time to jettison everything we know about working together? Of course not. That would be to once again think in terms of compartments: the old ways of working together go out the window as we embrace the latest ideas, time and again. It is precisely this reflex that makes us surf from one trend to another in a manic search for ways to change the world. As already mentioned, the ME-WE principle is a general intention that can be spliced on to existing systems to provide an extra dimension.

Today, we live and work in two different "models": one that is overwhelmingly focused on structure and another that is directed at culture. Since these models are the roots from which our future grows, we must not overlook them. In fact, with the future in mind, it is well worth the effort of placing them in the proper perspective.

> THE ME-WE PRINCIPLE IS A GENERAL INTENTION THAT CAN BE SPLICED ON TO EXISTING SYSTEMS TO PROVIDE AN EXTRA DIMENSION.

TOP-DOWN MODEL: STRUCTURE CREATES ORDER

When the Second World War ended, the world needed fresh energy if it was to rise again from the rubble. We looked for clear, unambiguous structures that people could rely on. We know this structure as the top-down model. All walks of life were organised by a narrow top layer and implemented by a broad base.

To connect the two levels, there was a highly organised civil society where people pooled their resources. They derived their identity from the group to which they belonged. You were a worker, employer (boss) or farmer. You did your job, organised to demand your rights, believed in systems, church and state and thus rebuilt your world. There was trust and there were clear agreements.

Naturally, movements came and went that were at odds with the bosses and the governments. For example, in 1968, worldwide protests were aimed at traditional power structures and set in motion closer consultation between the workers and the powers-that-be. But the structure of society remained essentially the same. We see that many veterans of May '68 ended up as managers in very mainstream top-down organisations. There was a lot of opportunity in that period. Society appeared to be malleable because it had such a clear and orderly structure.

CULTURE MODEL: EVERYONE IS A LEADER

The last turn of the century was accompanied by the usual nervousness and urge to transform. A new technological revolution and a number of crises following on each other's heels turned the "secure" structures of the post-war period on their heads: the government did not appear to be able to protect us any more, banks went bankrupt and religion lost its moral superiority. Since then, a highly individualised, functionally driven economy has stepped in to make its mark on our everyday lives.

Whereas groups of people were emancipated in the post-war period, today it is the individual who emancipates him- or herself. Ever since the millennium, we have become unique people with unique desires and dreams. The focus has moved away from structures and towards "me" feeling good. In the same way, organisational models that no longer focus on hierarchy but instead on a culture of cooperation are gaining ground.

WHEREAS GROUPS OF PEOPLE WERE EMANCIPATED IN THE POST-WAR PERIOD, TODAY IT IS THE INDIVIDUAL WHO EMANCIPATES HIM- OR HERSELF.

In this system, a very personal approach is employed that encourages people to take independent initiatives. Leadership is not seen as a top-down concept any more but instead as the responsibility of each person. Structures grow from the inside out rather than from above. The boss of earlier times becomes the facilitator who is mainly concerned with monitoring values so that a strong, connected culture emerges.

STIPULATIONS

The structural system had the advantage of clarity. We could build our world relatively quickly due to unmistakable agreements and expectations. The culture system places much more emphasis on our personal sense of responsibility and the connection between individuals. If we marry the simplicity of one system with the reciprocity of the other, we make great strides. Because the power of today's culture system is that it uses values such as authenticity, transparency and accountability as guidelines for cooperation. They just need to be converted into clear agreements and objectives.

Older models of cooperation have proved their worth: they offered order in chaos. But you will have noticed that the ME-WE principle hails from quite another line of thought: it does not aim to impose order. Logical order is simply the natural result of applying the principle. When you do so, you automatically evolve a sort of organic equilibrium. It does not have to be forced through some carefully planned system.

So this does not make existing models superfluous but it does bring them down to size: they should not be used to organise or regulate everything in the world. Instead, they express a number of practical stipulations and procedures that make it easier for us to live and work together according to a simple principle.

—

CHARISMATIC
ENGAGEMENT

PARTICIPATORY
RESPONSIBILITY

**PERPETUUM
MOBILE
OF STRONG
CONNECTIONS**

When you apply the first two steps, individually or as a group, you trigger a perpetual motion machine of ever-stronger connections to yourself and the rest of the world. First you silence the noise of daily life by asking yourself about your inner inspiration. And in the process of finding out, you tap into forgotten energy sources in yourself. By releasing them, you become more self-aware and confident. It is as if you have grown deeper roots that penetrate directly into your vitality.

This accelerating power enables you to better understand reality. You feel like a more important part of the world and experience how what is good for someone else is also good

for you. And vice versa. With this intention, you try to build your life, are curious and demonstrate interest in the people, ideas and innovations that you encounter on a daily basis. But you do not allow others to write your scenario. You use these impulses to increase your lust for life and to confront the parts of you that are still under the surface.

Since this dynamic links personal with societal growth, the whole world and all the opportunities it offers become your playing field. You notice that you experience fewer and fewer impediments to your growth and evolution. No mental, emotional or physical obstacles. Your life becomes a creative fount of possibility and opportunity so that you can make the best of yourself and your environment.

YOUR LIFE BECOMES A CREATIVE FOUNT OF POSSIBILITY AND OPPORTUNITY SO THAT YOU CAN MAKE THE BEST OF YOURSELF AND YOUR ENVIRONMENT.

A perpetual movement of deepening and broadening develops. The more firmly you are grounded, the more fully and creatively you can engage with the world and even integrate it into who you are.

—

THE FIVE-STEP REFLEX

In this book, we described five steps that can help you to keep up your "perpetual motion" of permanent growth, day after day. The steps can be practised limitlessly and applied very concretely in your life, and will rapidly become a reflex:

Step 1: Plunge into your deeper perspective
Ask yourself what inspires and motivates you to do what you do and allow your entire "system" to answer.

Step 2: Observe and accept
Register any information or injured feelings that surface. Accept all the emotions that surround these feelings.

Step 3: Apply the ME-WE principle
Connect with your environment and search for gain in everything you do: for yourself, your personal and professional relations and all of society.

Step 4: Use your enhanced consciousness to engage
Be aware of the people and situations that you attract.
Try out new experiences.

Step 5: Start all over again
Examine how your experiences are affecting you, how
you are reacting and what sort of situations and circumstances you are ending up in. And start again with the
first step.

You discover that commitment to yourself is the same as
commitment to your surroundings. When you nourish the
roots, the crown of the tree is bigger, stronger and more
beautiful. And more people are attracted to it and to the
fruits that it yields.

However, this dynamic does not come without strings attached. You are stepping into a very delicate equilibrium.
Look at it as a sort of universal ecosystem that is destroyed
by the slightest disturbance. You don't develop a charisma
that you can appropriate and hang on to. This would not
make sense anyway, since it would mean that you are trying

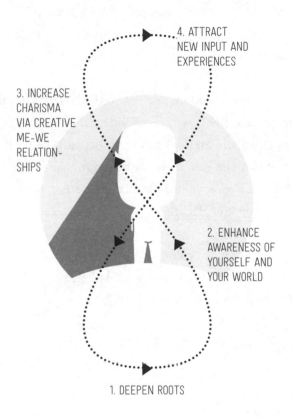

4. ATTRACT
NEW INPUT AND
EXPERIENCES

3. INCREASE
CHARISMA
VIA CREATIVE
ME-WE
RELATION-
SHIPS

2. ENHANCE
AWARENESS OF
YOURSELF AND
YOUR WORLD

1. DEEPEN ROOTS

to put something in a box again. What you do create is a sort of aura that draws people to you who are both self-sufficient and helpful to you. You attract positive situations that you could never have imagined before and create opportunities that make life a richer experience. When you tap into your charismatic engagement, you see your life and your world transform.

There are a few important responsibilities attached if you are to protect and maintain this equilibrium. After all, when you realise that there are no boundaries between yourself and the world around you, there are bound to be ramifications. The following three come immediately to mind, each one on a different relational level:

- Be consistent and vulnerable
- Find the emotion behind every relationship
- Try to see the world as it is

―

BE CONSISTENT AND VULNERABLE

Charisma is obviously a nice thing. Your new self-awareness and the connections that you make as a result provide you with a new "status", as it were, and a more powerful presence. It hardly needs saying that your ego will swell and there will be a part of you that wallows in the affirmation and attention that you receive. There is nothing wrong with this per se. We do not have to feel guilty about feeling good or getting well-deserved pats on the back.

But herein lies the danger. You may lose yourself in this unfamiliar "status" and then return to the pigeonholing habit from which you just escaped. By identifying with the compartment that the world places you in, you trap yourself in a new conviction. This is where people can go wrong. Having mined new creativity from within themselves, they then use this on the surface as fuel for exclusively personal gain. They instantly draw attention, surround themselves with supporters and are clearly enjoying success. However, this is counterproductive and even harmful as it is far from a balanced, win-win situation. You are using your energy to take even more from other people.

> YOU MAY LOSE YOURSELF IN THIS UNFAMILIAR "STATUS" AND THEN RETURN TO THE PIGEONHOLING HABIT FROM WHICH YOU JUST ESCAPED.

So, when someone steps into the participatory dynamic, they can use their new energy to damage people and to superficially bolster themselves. But the effect can only be short-term because you are actually disempowering yourself. This behaviour does not lead to contentment or happiness since it reattaches the meaning of your life to external perceptions – the opposite of your innermost self. You may notice that you are perhaps regarded as successful above the surface but that you do not feel happier. In response, you may find yourself striving for even more superficial success and becoming even more exhausted in the process of trying to achieve something that is actually alien to your soul. And then you end up right back where you started.

Does this mean that we have to be perfect in our approach? That we must never deviate from the path and commit ourselves to wearing a holier-than-thou straitjacket of self-discipline? Of course not, that would be unlivable and doomed to failure. The secret does not lie in the perfection of the path but in recognising its imperfection. When you are aware of the pitfalls and can deal with them in an open and vulnerable way, are prepared to admit them to the people around you, then you are more likely to stay connected to your source of inspiration. We can only progress by being open and consistent about the principles inherent to our growth and development from a vulnerable human perspective. This is a

THE SECRET DOES NOT LIE IN THE
PERFECTION OF THE PATH BUT IN
RECOGNISING ITS IMPERFECTION.
WHEN YOU ARE AWARE OF THE PIT-
FALLS AND CAN DEAL WITH THEM
IN AN OPEN AND VULNERABLE WAY,
THEN YOU ARE MORE LIKELY TO
STAY CONNECTED TO YOUR SOURCE
OF INSPIRATION.

human trajectory so it can only work by a process of trying and failing.

When your environment makes the appearance of the contrary, then you need to pop the bubble of perfection that surrounds you. Especially in your work environment. We are human and therefore enjoy the privilege of learning from repeatedly humbling experiences - so that we can live more intensely.

WHEN YOUR ENVIRON-
MENT MAKES THE
APPEARANCE OF THE
CONTRARY, THEN YOU
NEED TO POP THE
BUBBLE OF PERFECTION
THAT SURROUNDS YOU.

The president of a large, successful organisation developed a very people- and community-oriented corporate culture. He built an efficient organisation by placing a strong emphasis on good cooperation practices and by inviting his personnel to embark on personal learning trajectories. He never had problems attracting new talent: people wanted to come and work for him. The man was idolised and had over five hundred people eating out of his hand. He seemed to be perceived as almost a guru by some of his staff. And then he suffered a personal setback: a malignant tumour was found in his body.

Fortunately, the diagnosis was made at an early stage of the disease. After undergoing a simple procedure, he could, if he wished, simply continue to work without his employees even noticing that anything was wrong. There were those in his management team who believed that the president should keep his "problem" under wraps so as not to imperil the stability of the organisation. Surely he, the visionary, needed to appear strong and steadfast? What if people were to find out that their "model" was in fact highly vulnerable? In the eyes of some, the man had become the personification of the organisation's success.

After thinking it over for a while, he took the right decision: he told his family, followed by his personnel. He explained what had happened, what emotions it had triggered in him and what the recovery process would entail. The news came like a bombshell to his employees. But it also brought about a new dimension to the corporate culture. There was no question of the staff feeling insecure or destabilised. On the contrary. The calm support that the man received from them was utterly touching. He felt no sense of isolation during his period of hospitalisation and rehabilitation.

THE NEWS CAME LIKE A BOMBSHELL TO HIS EMPLOYEES. BUT IT ALSO BROUGHT ABOUT A NEW DIMENSION TO THE CORPORATE CULTURE.

Along with this support came an outpouring of personal stories. People found it easier to share their own experiences of dealing with illness and mortality, which only served to strengthen bonds. They barely knew about each other's personal circumstances before, despite the fact that they had worked together for a long time. A lot of hidden realities surfaced. It also meant that from now on, when someone was on long-term sick leave, they could expect overt support from their colleagues. Work would have to be put on hold for a while, but not the friendships and connections. Furthermore, many felt that this was in fact what helped them to get back on their feet.

—

FIND THE EMOTION BEHIND EVERY RELATIONSHIP

When you endeavour to live and work in a participative way, you uncover an emotion in yourself and in your environment. It is exciting to become aware of this and to keep seeking the emotion that exists behind the world as we know it. You will become more sensitive to non-mental language; to whatever cannot be put into precise words but still leaves an impression. Music, poetry, art, a good film, a fascinating television series or a chance encounter can all provoke deep emotions. They speak to the unconscious, non-rational side of you and can offer a direct line to your innermost self. That is why it can be so difficult to rationally explain why something has touched you. This is wonderful. Art cannot save the world, but it does help you understand the world inside of you.

> ART CANNOT SAVE THE WORLD, BUT IT DOES HELP YOU UNDERSTAND THE WORLD INSIDE OF YOU.

It is fascinating to realise that you become more sensitive in your daily life to the intrinsic emotions that guide people's words and actions. You learn to gauge better what is behind the words they speak by regularly delving below your own surface and approaching life from the win-win perspective. You learn how to interpret and comprehend the emotional language behind the words. This results in a far more nuanced and dense picture of the situations in which you find yourself.

You can practise this skill by simply deciding to not only listen to words but to the emotions that are hidden behind them. You will be amazed by how much feeling there is on the surface of every conversation. We are just no longer accustomed to seeing it. When you notice and articulate your own and your interlocutor's emotions, you understand each other's reality and the relationship you build is a more nourishing one. The more you do this, the easier it becomes and the more you can "see" and judge the situation. This is particularly helpful when you feel trapped in something. You can perceive and experience so much more in a situation if you open up your own subconscious and are receptive to the people around you.

> *A local politician was finding it difficult to deal with her constituents constantly approaching her on the street, in the shops and on the market square to talk about the asylum centre that was about to open in their town. This was in a region where many international war refugees were seeking shelter. She suffered a daily dose of arguments such as "These people should stay in their own country", "There are already enough of them here" and "I don't understand why you favour foreigners over the poor in your own country".*

The woman felt physically ill from having to listen to all these kneejerk reactions. Whenever she tried to explain her standpoint, which she clearly stated as a belief in solidarity between people, she encountered an even bigger wall of outrage. It completely exhausted her and led to her questioning her own political and social commitment.

During an exercise, we examined the entire situation and not only the mental, rational aspect that saw her and her constituents relentlessly at odds. We asked her to take some distance from the situation and ask herself about the emotions that lay behind the words they used. And then to think about her own emotions. She instantly responded with 'It's obvious. The people are frightened. They're afraid that their world is changing and becoming less safe.' She expressed her own underlying emotion as impotence, the sense that she could not do what the people who elected her wanted her to do. And she also realised in that moment that there was no point in judging public opinion, let alone the emotions that led to it. That would only result in more argument.

WHENEVER SHE TRIED TO EXPLAIN HER STANDPOINT, WHICH SHE CLEARLY STATED AS A BELIEF IN SOLIDARITY BETWEEN PEOPLE, SHE ENCOUNTERED AN EVEN BIGGER WALL OF OUTRAGE.

From the moment that she deployed these insights in

conversations with locals, exchanges became more nuanced and personal. When she asked searching questions about her interlocutor's fears and expressed her own feeling of powerlessness, rewarding exchanges followed during which both felt understood as opposed to defensive. This allowed an atmosphere of mutual trust to grow and for solutions to be sought together.

We often work on this during our coaching sessions for companies and organisations. Role-playing helps people practise and is interesting and exciting. Who would not want to learn how to see, live and work with a clearer mind?

———

TRY TO SEE THE WORLD AS IT IS

Finally, try to see the world as it really is, not as it is shown to you. When you look at the world from your deeper perspective, you gradually develop a different view of it. You try to see beyond the superficiality of everyday illusions. The illusions are created to counteract the overwhelming stimuli to which we are subjected and which leave us feeling confused about what we are supposed to believe.

The fast pace of our daily lives means that we actually only see fragments of reality, which flash by like an express train. We create a vision of the world based on these brief and superficial impressions. These impressions are then reinforced by the belief system of the environment in which we find ourselves. You know the feeling: in some circles, your views on ways to interpret reality may not be welcome at all. You can find yourself in a belief cluster where people collect as many little pieces of information as they can to confirm that their way of seeing reality is the right one. You come across this during election campaigns: people rally around candidates and often accept as truth the most absurd statements - if only to make sure that the reality in which they have invested does not collapse. When you stir this into the mix of fear and manipulation that issues from ambitions of power, then you have the ingredients for the extremely dangerous cocktail called mass hysteria. And this leads people into a fictional world of pure, unadulterated madness.

When you adopt the participatory approach, you notice that you start to detach yourself more easily and quickly from the bombardment of fleeting information and the belief clusters in which you sometimes find yourself. Or, to put it more succinctly, you begin to experience it all as what it is: fragments and clusters of a larger truth. So you learn to look at the world in another way. You slowly become able to absorb what is actually occurring. Your view of what you observe becomes more honest and less coloured by the filters through which facts pass before reaching you. You become motivated to learn the truth behind the reality. It is just the same as how you learn to look for the deeper dimension in the world around you once you have plumbed your own depths. You feel compelled to look again to see what is really going on.

YOU LEARN TO LOOK AT THE WORLD IN ANOTHER WAY. YOU SLOWLY BECOME ABLE TO ABSORB WHAT IS ACTUALLY OCCURRING.

If something is of real interest to you, you make the effort to collect all the scraps of information and wash them of the layers of opinion that have muddied the truth. Furthermore, you attempt to contextualise all the quotes and slogans that are flying around in the ether. This brings you closer to the real heart of matters. (News sources that constrain themselves to reporting facts have a great future ahead of them: there are enough opinions, some seven billion of them, but it is the actualities that are increasingly fascinating.) The more facts and context you gather, the easier it is to take a standpoint. You use who you are and where you are in your life and work as a yardstick. You test facts against your own intuition, roots and personality. An idea thus forms that is entirely yours and that could potentially affect the world. You prepare yourself to test it in a real-life scenario.

When you do this, you soon find yourself at odds with prevailing opinion. Because you are rejecting opinion-forming based on bits and pieces of truth and instead are trying to see what is real. Of course, you cannot magically liberate yourself from the habit of imbibing the pieces of news that you are fed, but you can debunk information to yourself and the people around you.

Political debates are a great example of how intellectual toing and froing can degenerate into mud-slinging matches. There is nothing wrong in itself with sharing views and opinions with politicians on the opposite side. But as spectators, we often have the impression that we are watching gladiators armed with oneliners fighting it out in an arena.

AS SPECTATORS, WE OFTEN HAVE THE IMPRESSION THAT WE ARE WATCHING GLADIATORS ARMED WITH ONELINERS FIGHTING IT OUT IN AN ARENA.

The point is simply to win the debate. One wonders why it is even necessary. Fewer and fewer people find it a salubrious spectacle.

If a politician were to ask me for advice, I would practise with them ways to avoid getting caught up in that type of classic debate: to display instead genuine interest in the actual message that the other politician is trying to convey (and the underlying emotion). Perhaps it would be an idea to insert an item in every televised political debate that tasks politicians with expressing what they could learn from each other. And the areas of agreement that would allow them to really help society.

———

TIME FOR ACTION

The transition period that we are currently going through in the economy and society is one of great uncertainty and confusion. There is a new kind of warfare being waged around the world. Large multinationals are more powerful than ever before. Politics is searching for its grassroots and usually getting bogged down in day-to-day issues. The media is trying to strike a balance between rating figures, power and objectivity. Religious systems are looking for more breathing space. And a large faction of the financial world is probably heading straight for the next crisis of values. We can all sense this and it makes us look carefully at new ways to cope in these precarious times.

When working with people and companies, one notices a prevailing feeling that "something" is wrong and fundamentally in need of changing. There is a growing willingness to listen to what at first seem to be rather alternative solutions, such as participatory entrepreneurship. We often hear people express relief that there is a totally different way of looking at oneself and reality and that this perspective actually feels very obvious and instinctive.

Hence the call for anyone who enters into this dynamic to always seek the calm and participatory perspective in their work and life. This mindset is anything but bland or woolly: it keeps the essence of our being in an affable, peaceful and connected equilibrium. This not only provides us with the fearlessness necessary to experience and assimilate our acrimonious society but also to transform it into a creative force. A perspective that places us at the heart of the daily debates that often polarise our lives and work, in order to show that they are a projection of one and the same reality. Where we supplement the rational with feeling. Where we seek the middle way every time because that is where everyone wants essentially the same thing, dreams of the same thing and recognises their place in the world.

THIS MINDSET IS ANYTHING BUT BLAND OR WOOLLY: IT KEEPS THE ESSENCE OF OUR BEING IN AN AFFABLE, PEACEFUL AND CONNECTED EQUILIBRIUM.

Today, there is more experimentation with ways to infuse reason with feeling in our daily lives than ever before. A national radio station recently launched a week-long search for ideas to make lasting changes to the economy and society. The project set out to formulate real advice for politicians from the citizens on various facets of society. It was wonderful to see how many ideas and suggestions flooded in that bypassed the mental to probe much deeper into emotions as a resource for areas of agreement. For example, the programme invited ministers to hold talks from a place of quiet contemplation. It experimented with singing together so that harmony could be felt rather than needing to be repeatedly argued. All sorts of methods like these were trialled, creating fascinating radio, but the experience also showed how much people crave more substantial and profound thought pieces from the media, indicating a desire for more conscious lives.

STAY IN THE MIDDLEGROUND, LOOK FOR EQUILIBRIUM. OBSERVE THE EXTREMES BUT ONLY SO THAT YOU ARE FAMILIAR WITH THEM. NOT AS SOMETHING BY WHICH TO DEFINE - LET ALONE IDENTIFY - YOURSELF.

There is no point in involving oneself in angry, rationalist debate. Stay in the middleground, look for equilibrium. Observe the extremes but only so that you are familiar with them. Not as something by which to define - let alone identify - yourself. Disseminate calm from an understanding of yourself and as a product of your constant effort to be yourself as fully as possible - in unison with the people around you. When one grounds oneself in the participatory spirit, one can find and then spread peace and level-headedness in the midst of chaos. A conscious and egalitarian investment in yourself on the one hand, and in the world on the other, offers the hope of stability. In times of crisis and great uncertainty, it is even more likely that it will be the people, organisations and companies espousing the participatory dynamic - a conscious investment in both themselves and the world - that will provide the much-needed foundation.

———

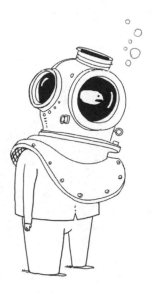

www.yourworkandyourlife.com

BIS Publishers
Building Het Sieraad
Postjesweg 1
1057 DT Amsterdam
The Netherlands
T +31 (0)20 515 02 30
bis@bispublishers.com
www.bispublishers.com

ISBN 978 90 6369 469 2
Copyright © 2016 Krist Pauwels and BIS Publishers

Design: choco cvba
Illustrations: Zaza
Translation: Heidi Steffes

www.choco.coop
www.yourworkandyourlife.com